I Was LABELED, BUT It Didn't Define Me

By: Miss Yolanda Renee Hill

Copyright © 2025 by Yolanda Hill

All rights reserved. This book or any portion thereof may not be reproduced or used in any manner whatsoever without the express written permission of the publisher except for the use of brief quotations in a book review.

Printed in the United States of America

First Edition, 2025

PAPERBACK ISBN: 979-8-3494-1763-4

EBOOK ISBN: 979-8-3494-1764-1

Red Pen Edits and Consulting

www.redpeneditsllc.com

TABLE OF CONTENTS

DEDICATIONS 1

INTRODUCTION 3

CHAPTER 1
   The Hill Family 5

CHAPTER 2
   Big Sister, Second Mother 9

CHAPTER 3
   Faith in the Living Room 13

CHAPTER 4
   A Preacher's Daughter 15

CHAPTER 5
   Finding My Place in the Family 19

CHAPTER 6
   Starting School 23

CHAPTER 7
   Overcoming Labels 27

CHAPTER 8
> A Mother's Strength 31

CHAPTER 9
> Embracing My Purpose 33

CHAPTER 10
> Trusting in God's Timing 37

CHAPTER 11
> The Power of Prayer 41

CHAPTER 12
> Embracing Change 45

CHAPTER 13
> Finding Strength in Struggles 49

CHAPTER 14
> Walking in Faith 53

CHAPTER 15
> Overcoming Fear 57

CHAPTER 16
> Living with Purpose 61

CHAPTER 17
The Beauty of Forgiveness 65

CHAPTER 18
Embracing God's Timing 69

CHAPTER 19
Strength in Weakness 73

CHAPTER 20
Walking in Victory 77

RESOURCES 89

ABOUT THE AUTHOR 91

DEDICATIONS

This book is dedicated to my mother, Sarah D. Hill. Thank you for encouraging me throughout my years of schooling and my entire life.

This book is also dedicated to all individuals who have special needs and may be going through similar situations.

INTRODUCTION

From the moment I could walk, talk, and dream, the world seemed eager to hand me labels—none of which I asked for. *Too much. Too loud. Too sensitive. Not enough.* These words, and others like them, clung to me like shadows, whispered behind my back and sometimes spoken boldly to my face. Teachers, peers, even well-meaning family members tried to write the script of my life before I ever got a chance to hold the pen.

But this book isn't about staying stuck in those labels. It's about defying them.

I know what it feels like to be underestimated, misunderstood, and misjudged. To be told who you are before you've had the chance to figure it out for yourself. I know the sting of rejection and the ache of believing, even for a moment, that those voices might be right.

Yet somewhere deep inside, I also knew I was born for more.

This is my story of breaking through the walls others tried to build around me. It's about rising when I was expected to shrink, and claiming victory in a life that many thought would be limited by other people's expectations. Through faith, resilience, fierce determination, and a refusal to give up, I learned to redefine my identity—not by what was said about me, but by what I knew to be true within me.

If you've ever been labeled, boxed in, or told you weren't enough, this book is for you. You don't have to be who they said you were. You don't have to live by anyone else's narrative.

You were born to break the mold.

And this is how I broke mine.

CHAPTER 1
The Hill Family

> *"Behold, how good and how pleasant it is for brethren to dwell together in unity!"*
>
> **Psalm 133:1**

I was born on July 3, 1973, to Sarah D. Hill and Benjamin F. Hill, the proud parents of 11 children. As the oldest, my life was anything but dull. Growing up in a big family was a blessing filled with laughter, lessons, and love. There was never a quiet moment in the Hill household, but those moments taught me about responsibility and resilience.

From an early age, I became the "second mother" to my siblings. They called me "Big Sister," but the name carried more meaning than they realized. It meant being the one to set an example, offer guidance, and lend a helping hand. Whether it was helping with homework, fixing a quick snack, or breaking up little squabbles, I was always there for my brothers and sisters.

My father, Benjamin, was a preacher at Greater Highway Deliverance Temple where Bishop Liston Page Sr, is the Pastor, and my mother, Sarah, was a missionary. Together, they raised us with a foundation rooted in faith and love. Every night at 8:00 p.m., we gathered in the living room for Bible study and prayer. Those moments were sacred. My father would read scriptures, and my mother would lead us in songs of praise. I still hear their voices echoing in my heart today.

One of my favorite memories was when my siblings and I would sing behind my father when he preached. We practiced in the front room, laughing, harmonizing, and sometimes just playing around. But when it was time to sing in church, we sang with all our hearts, knowing it brought joy to God and our parents.

Our parents taught us the value of working together. When Mommy went grocery shopping, Daddy stayed home to keep an eye on us. When she came back, we all pitched in to carry the bags inside. I remember those trips to the kitchen, hands full of grocery bags, laughing and teasing each other as we unloaded the week's food.

Sometimes, while my parents were out, my siblings would look to me for food. At first, I could only make peanut butter and jelly crackers or sometimes we'd mix ketchup and mayo pretending it was pizza, laughing as we savored our makeshift treat. But one day, when I was 19, my parents came home to find I'd cooked a real meal. My mother said, *"I know you're not messing up my food out the freezer!"* But when she tasted what I'd made, she smiled and said, *"My baby can cook!"* From that moment, she started letting me help in the kitchen, and I found a new sense of pride in contributing to the family. Those moments with Mommy, learning how to season, stir, and bake, became precious memories.

> **REFLECTION**
>
> *My parents' unwavering faith and strong leadership kept our family close-knit through it all. They taught us to lean on God in every season of life. As Proverbs 22:6 says, "Train up a child in the way he should go: and when he is old, he will not depart from it." This was the foundation my parents laid for us, and it continues to guide me today.*

CHAPTER 2
Big Sister, Second Mother

"Bear ye one another's burdens, and so fulfill the law of Christ."

Galatians 6:2

Growing up as the oldest of 11 siblings was both a blessing and a challenge. From the moment my younger brothers and sisters were born, I knew my role in the family went beyond just being a sibling, I was their protector, their cheerleader, and often, their stand-in mother.

They looked up to me in everything I did, and I took that responsibility seriously. My siblings called me "Big Sister" when we were younger, but as we grew older, the nickname changed to "Second Mother." At first, I didn't understand the weight of those words, but as the years went by, I realized it was a title of respect and love. In our bustling household, there was always something going on. My parents taught us to work together, meaning chores were never done alone. Whether folding clothes, cleaning the house, or looking after the younger ones, we all pitched in.

Being the "second mother" also meant being a role model. My parents often reminded me that my actions would set the tone for my younger siblings. "Yolanda," my mother would say, "they're watching you. Show them how to live right." Those words stayed with me, shaping how I carried myself. I wanted my siblings to see someone who was kind, responsible, and faithful to God.

We didn't have much, but we had each other. When we sang together behind my father during church services, it wasn't just about the music, it was about unity. Those moments that we'd practice taught me the power of working together and supporting one another.

As the eldest, I also had to navigate the balance between authority and love. There were times when I had to correct my siblings, and other times when I had to be their confidante. I learned to listen, to guide without judgment, and to encourage them to be their best selves.

> **REFLECTION**
>
> *Looking back, I see how God was preparing me for leadership, even in those small moments. He gave me a heart for service and a love for my family that continues to this day.*
>
> *As Galatians 6:2 reminds us, carrying one another's burdens is an act of love, and I am grateful for the opportunity to have done that for my siblings.*

CHAPTER 3
Faith in the Living Room

> *"Train up a child in the way he should go: and when he is old, he will not depart from it."*
>
> **Proverbs 22:6**

In the Hill household, faith wasn't just something we talked about on Sundays; it was a part of our everyday lives. No matter what the day held, we always gathered at 8 p.m. to have family devotion. It was the anchor that held us together. My father, Benjamin F. Hill, a preacher, and my mother, Sarah D. Hill, a missionary, made sure that we stayed rooted in God's Word.

Our nightly devotion was essential, Daddy would reach the scriptures and explain the meaning behind each verse.

As children, we didn't always understand the depth of what we were learning, but those moments left an impression on our hearts. I remember one night when Daddy read Philippians 4:13: *"I can do all things through Christ who strengthens me."* That verse became a cornerstone in my life, reminding me that no challenge was too big for God to handle.

CHAPTER 4
A Preacher's Daughter

> *"Let your light so shine before men, that they may see your good works, and glorify your Father which is in heaven."*
>
> **Matthew 5:16**

Growing up as the daughter of a preacher wasn't always easy, but it was always meaningful. My father, Benjamin F. Hill, was a man of few words, but his actions spoke volumes. He was a quiet encourager, always reminding us to stay focused and to lean on God in everything we did.

When Daddy preached, it was powerful. His words carried wisdom and truth, touching the hearts of everyone who listened. My siblings and I often accompanied him to church services, and we sang as part of the worship. Those moments were special—standing behind my father, singing songs of praise, and feeling the presence of God move through the congregation.

When it was time to sing in church, we gave it our all. I can still see my father's proud smile as we stood behind him, our voices blending in harmony.

My mother, Sarah, was just as devoted to the church. As a missionary, she carried a deep passion for serving others. Her faith was unshakable, and her dedication to God was an example for all of us. She always reminded us that our lives were meant to glorify God and to fulfill His purpose.

Being raised in a home where faith was central taught me the importance of living a life that reflects God's love. My parents didn't just preach the Word; they lived it. They taught us to pray, to trust God in all things, and to seek His guidance in every decision.

I remember one evening when Daddy sat us down and shared this verse: *"The steps of a good man are ordered by the Lord: and he delighteth in his way"* (Psalm 37:23). He explained that when we follow God's plan for our lives, we'll find peace and purpose. Those words stayed with me, shaping the way I approached every challenge and opportunity.

> **REFLECTION**
>
> *As I look back on those years, I'm grateful for the foundation my parents gave me. Their faith and guidance taught me that no matter what labels the world tries to place on you, God has the final say. As Matthew 5:16 reminds us, our light is meant to shine, reflecting God's goodness to the world.*

CHAPTER 5
Finding My Place in the Family

> *"For I know the plans I have for you," declares the Lord, "plans to prosper you and not to harm you, plans to give you hope and a future."*
>
> **Jeremiah 29:11**

In a family with 11 siblings, it could have been easy to feel lost in the crowd, but my parents made sure each of us knew we had a purpose. Even as the eldest, I sometimes struggled to find my place. Was I just the big sister? Or was I meant for something more? These questions stayed with me throughout my childhood and into adulthood.

Being the oldest came with responsibilities that shaped me. I learned to lead by example, to put others' needs before my own, and to guide my siblings with love. My parents trusted me to help when they weren't around, and that trust gave me confidence. Yet, it also came with pressure. I worried that if I made a mistake, I'd disappoint them or let my siblings down.

One memory that stands out is a time when my youngest siblings got into a little trouble while our parents were out. They had been running around the house, knocking things over, and making a mess. I tried to calm them down, but nothing seemed to work. When Mommy and Daddy got home, I braced myself for their disappointment. Instead, my father simply said, "Yolanda, you did your best. It's not about perfection, it's about trying with love."

His words reminded me that my role wasn't to be perfect; it was to be present. As Jeremiah 29:11 assures us, God's plans for us are filled with hope and purpose, even when we feel uncertain or overwhelmed.

Over time, I began to embrace my unique role in the family. I wasn't just "big sister" or "second mother"—I was Yolanda, a young woman learning and growing alongside her siblings. I found joy in helping them with homework, teaching them life skills, and cheering them on in their achievements. Watching them succeed reminded me that my role wasn't just about responsibility; it was about love and support.

> **REFLECTION**
>
> *In every family, each person plays a part, and every part is significant. I realized that God placed me as the eldest for a reason. It wasn't always easy, but it was a blessing. My journey of finding my place taught me that God's plans are always greater than we can imagine, and they're meant to shape us into who He's called us to be.*

CHAPTER 6
Starting School

"And let us not be weary in well doing: for in due season we shall reap, if we faint not."

Galatians 6:9

In 1978, my educational journey began when I entered kindergarten. I was excited, nervous, and ready to learn. But little did I know, this journey would be filled with both challenges and triumphs that would shape me into the person I am today.

I WAS LABELED BUT IT DIDN'T DEFINE ME

At 5 years old, I was eager to make new friends and soak up knowledge. I loved my kindergarten teacher and enjoyed the songs, crafts, and stories we shared in class. But despite my enthusiasm, I struggled to keep up. By the end of the year, I learned I'd have to repeat kindergarten.

At 6 years old, repeating kindergarten wasn't easy. I felt like I had let myself down. When I moved to first grade, the struggles continued. Math, reading, and other subjects seemed more difficult for me than for my classmates. By the end of first grade, I failed again.

It was hard to watch my siblings excel while I stayed behind. When report cards came, I dreaded hearing the results. My siblings' cards were filled with A's and B's, while mine was covered in red marks. I began to feel like I wasn't smart enough and that school wasn't for me.

My parents, however, never gave up on me. My mother, Sarah, would sit me down with books and say, "No TV for you. Go read, and when you're done, tell me what you learned." At the time, I didn't appreciate her persistence, but looking back, I know it was her way of teaching me discipline and resilience.

At 8 years old, things started to change. I was still in first grade but finally began to catch on to some of the lessons. My classmates nicknamed me "Tall Tree" because I was taller than everyone else in the room. Though the name stung at first, it became a reminder that standing out wasn't always a bad thing.

When I entered second grade at 9 years old, I passed with flying colors. For the first time, I felt a sense of accomplishment in school. I realized I wasn't "dumb" as I had thought, I just needed time and support to learn in my own way.

REFLECTION

Galatians 6:9 reminds us not to grow weary in welldoing, for in due time, we will reap the rewards of our efforts. My early school years taught me perseverance. No matter how many times I fell, God gave me the strength to get back up.

CHAPTER 7
Overcoming Labels

> *"But God hath chosen the foolish things of the world to confound the wise; and God hath chosen the weak things of the world to confound the things which are mighty."*
>
> **1 Corinthians 1:27**

At the age of 10, I was placed in special education classes. The school's child study team had determined that I had learning difficulties, and they labeled me as "mentally retarded." Hearing that label was devastating. It felt like the world had decided who I was before I even had a chance to show what I could do.

When I got home and told my parents, they refused to accept the negativity tied to that label. My mother opened the Bible to Philippians 4:13 and reminded me: *"I can do all things through Christ who strengthens me."* My father reassured me that God had a plan for my life, one far greater than any label.

Entering the special education program was intimidating at first. I was placed in a classroom with students of varying disabilities. Some of them couldn't read, while others struggled with math or writing. But instead of feeling discouraged, I found my purpose in helping others. I joined a group for students who could read, and I worked with my teacher's assistant to help those who were still learning.

Despite my progress, the stigma of being in special education followed me. I noticed how teachers treated us differently from other students. They would allow the general education kids to participate in fun activities while we stayed behind, reading or doing worksheets. It was as if the world had decided that we didn't deserve the same opportunities.

But I didn't let that discourage me. I paid attention, watching how others made things like scarves and blankets. I quietly taught myself by observing, and soon I was creating beautiful handmade items. It felt empowering to prove that I was capable of learning and excelling, even if it wasn't in the way others expected.

One day, a teacher pulled my mother aside in the hallway and said, "She's not going to have a life like you. She won't amount to anything if she doesn't figure out what to do for herself." Hearing those words hurt deeply. But my mother didn't flinch. She looked the teacher straight in the eyes and said, "God has already written her story, and you are not the author."

That moment became a turning point for me. My mother's faith reminded me that no one's opinion could define my worth. I was more than a label. I was a child of God, fearfully and wonderfully made (Psalm 139:14).

REFLECTION

The world may try to define you with labels. Still, God's purpose for your life surpasses every limitation. 1 Corinthians 1:27 reminds us that God often uses those deemed "weak" by the world to accomplish extraordinary things. Trust in His plan and never let anyone tell you what you can't do.

CHAPTER 8
A Mother's Strength

> *"Strength and honour are her clothing; and she shall rejoice in time to come."*
>
> **Proverbs 31:25**

My mother, Sarah D. Hill, was a woman of unwavering strength and faith. She didn't just talk about the power of prayer—she lives it. Through every trial and triumph, my mother's faith stood as a beacon of hope for all of us. She taught us that no matter how difficult life became, God was always with us.

I watched her face challenges head-on with a smile and unshakable faith. Raising 11 children wasn't easy, but she did it with grace. Even when things were tight financially, she made sure we had what we needed. She didn't just provide for us; she nurtured our spirits.

Circumstances that went into that meal made it feel abundant. I learned that it wasn't the quantity of what we had that mattered—it was the heart with which we gave thanks for it.

My mother's strength was evident not only in her prayers but in how she lived every day. She worked tirelessly, juggling household duties, teaching us about the Lord, and making sure we were ready for the future. She didn't just expect us to grow spiritually, she showed us how.

As I grew older, I understood more about the sacrifices she made for our family. She wasn't just a mother—she was a spiritual leader, a role model, and a teacher. Through her, I learned the power of faith and the importance of standing firm in God's promises.

REFLECTION

Proverbs 31:25 speaks of a woman of strength and honor, someone who faces life's challenges with confidence and rejoices in the future. My mother, Sarah, was the embodiment of this. She showed me that true strength comes from trusting in God and walking by faith, no matter the circumstance.

CHAPTER 9
Embracing My Purpose

> *"For I know the plans I have for you," declares the Lord, "plans to prosper you and not to harm you, plans to give you a hope and a future."*
>
> **Jeremiah 29:11**

As I navigated my way through school and life, I began to realize that God had a purpose for me, even though I didn't fully understand what that purpose was at the time. After years of struggling with school, being placed in special education classes, and feeling different from my peers, I came to understand that my journey wasn't an accident.

In 1982, when I passed the second grade with flying colors, something inside me shifted. I had always doubted myself, thinking that because I struggled in school, I wasn't capable of achieving great things. But that year, I began to see a glimpse of the person I was meant to become.

My mother always told me that God had plans for my life, and despite the labels I had received, I began to hold on to that promise. She taught me that our struggles are often a part of God's greater plan, a way to refine us and prepare us for the future He has in store.

One of the most profound lessons I learned was that God uses our challenges to bring us closer to Him. As I worked hard in school and overcame my doubts, I felt God's presence guiding me, urging me to keep moving forward. It wasn't always easy, but I knew I wasn't alone.

My purpose began to take shape as I realized that God had given me the gift of perseverance, the ability to keep going even when the path is tough. I learned to embrace the obstacles I faced, not as limitations, but as opportunities to grow and strengthen my faith.

REFLECTION

Jeremiah 29:11 assures us that God's plans for us are filled with hope and a future. Embracing my purpose meant trusting in His plan, even when I didn't understand it. Through every struggle, God was shaping me into who I was meant to be.

CHAPTER 10
Trusting in God's Timing

> *"To everything there is a season, and a time for every matter under heaven."*
>
> **Ecclesiastes 3:1**

As I walked through the years of my youth, I faced challenges that seemed insurmountable. There were moments when I felt like I was being held back, as if the doors to my future were closed, and I was stuck in a cycle of failure. But amid those difficult moments, I learned a powerful truth: God's timing is perfect.

There were times I questioned why things weren't happening the way I wanted. I wanted to succeed at school, excel in all that I did, and be just like my siblings, who seemed to breeze through life without struggle. But I quickly realized that everyone's journey is different.

In those moments of doubt, God reminded me that my struggles were not permanent. Ecclesiastes 3:1 tells us that there is a time for everything. Sometimes, we're in a season of preparation, where the lessons we need to learn don't come immediately. It may feel like we're stuck, but in truth, we're being shaped for what's ahead.

God's timing became more apparent as I looked back on the years that had passed. I realized that the challenges I faced in school and life were necessary to build my character, my faith, and my strength. Each setback was part of God's plan to prepare me for something greater.

I also learned that trusting in God's timing means letting go of the need to control every aspect of our lives. I had spent so many years trying to fix things on my own, striving for success in my strength. But it wasn't until I surrendered my plans to God that I began to see real growth.

When I fully trusted in God's timing, I began to see doors open that I never expected. Opportunities came when I least anticipated them. God had been working behind the scenes, and when the time was right, He revealed His plan.

> **REFLECTION**
>
> *Trusting in God's timing requires patience and faith. Ecclesiastes 3:1 reminds us that everything has its season. While we may not understand the delays or the struggles, we can trust that God is preparing us for the future He has planned.*

CHAPTER 11
The Power of Prayer

> *"The effective, fervent prayer of a righteous man avails much."*
>
> **James 5:16**

Throughout my life, prayer has been my constant companion. As a child, I remember my parents gathering us together every night for Bible study and prayer. My father, a preacher, would lead us in prayer, while my mother would offer words of encouragement and scriptures to guide us. Prayer was never just a ritual—it was a lifeline.

There were times when the weight of the world felt unbearable. The pressure to succeed, to be like my siblings, and to live up to everyone's expectations often overwhelmed me. But no matter how difficult life became, I always knew I could turn to God in prayer.

James 5:16 tells us that the prayer of a righteous person has great power. I learned early on that prayer wasn't just about asking God for things, it was about building a relationship with Him. In prayer, I could express my fears, my doubts, and my hopes. I could ask for guidance, strength, and wisdom. But most importantly, I could listen to God's voice.

I remember one particular moment in my life when I felt completely lost. I had struggled in school for so many years and had received so many labels that I began to question my worth.

But one night, I knelt beside my bed and poured out my heart to God. I asked Him to show me my purpose and to help me understand the path He had set before me.

In that moment, I felt a peace that transcended all understanding. God's presence surrounded me, and I knew that He had heard my prayer. It was as if a weight had been lifted from my shoulders, and I knew that no matter what happened, I was never alone.

From that day forward, prayer became more than just a routine, it became a source of strength and clarity. Whenever life became challenging, I would pray, and God would renew my spirit.

> **REFLECTION**
>
> *James 5:16 teaches us that prayer has power. It is a tool for strengthening our faith, seeking guidance, and finding peace in times of trouble. In my life, prayer has been the foundation that has carried me through even the most difficult times.*

CHAPTER 12
Embracing Change

"Behold, I will do a new thing; now it shall spring forth; shall ye not know it?"

Isaiah 43:19

Change is one of the few constants in life. Whether we want it or not, life has a way of shifting, growing, and moving us from one season to the next. For me, embracing change wasn't always easy, especially when it came to my personal growth and education.

Throughout my school years, I often felt like I was stuck in a pattern of struggle. Each year, I faced the same battles—feeling different, struggling with schoolwork, and trying to live up to the expectations of others. But what I didn't realize at the time was that God was using those challenges to prepare me for the changes He had planned.

Isaiah 43:19 says, *"Behold, I will do a new thing; now it shall spring forth; shall ye not know it?"* God's plan for my life was unfolding, and though I couldn't see it at the moment, He was leading me toward something greater. Every challenge, every failure, and every victory was a part of the process of transformation.

When I was placed in special education classes, I struggled to see how that would benefit me. But as time went on, I began to understand that the changes in my life were not setbacks but growth opportunities. I learned to adapt to new environments, to work harder than I ever had before, and to find new ways of doing things.

Embracing change meant letting go of the old ways of thinking and being open to the new things God was doing in my life. It meant trusting that, even in the face of uncertainty, God had a plan. I began to see each new day as an opportunity to grow, to learn, and to move closer to the person God had called me to be.

It wasn't easy. Change never is. But I learned that God doesn't always reveal His plans immediately. Sometimes, He asks us to take small steps, trusting that He is leading us toward a better future. As I embraced the changes in my life, I began to see the beautiful new things that God was doing in me.

> **REFLECTION**
>
> *Isaiah 43:19 reminds us that God is always doing something new. Change may be uncomfortable, but it is often the very thing that leads us to the next step in our journey. By embracing change, we allow God to work in our lives in powerful and transformative ways.*

CHAPTER 13
Finding Strength in Struggles

"We are hard pressed on every side, but not crushed; perplexed, but not in despair; persecuted, but not abandoned; struck down, but not destroyed."

2 Corinthians 4:8-9

Life is full of struggles. We can't escape them, no matter how hard we try. But one thing I've learned through my experiences is that our struggles don't *define* us, they *refine* us. They shape our character, strengthen our faith, and ultimately prepare us for the blessings God has in store.

From a young age, I faced many struggles. School was a constant challenge, especially when I was labeled as someone with learning difficulties. But the struggles didn't stop there. There were moments when I felt like I was fighting an uphill battle, facing obstacles that seemed impossible. Yet, it was during these moments that I began to see God's hand at work in my life.

2 Corinthians 4:8-9 describes the struggles we face but reminds us that we are not destroyed by them. We may feel pressed down, but we are not crushed. We may feel perplexed, but we are not in despair. We may feel struck down, but we are not destroyed. This scripture became a lifeline for me during the toughest times in my life.

As I looked back on the struggles I had faced, I began to realize that they had made me stronger. I learned to persevere, to keep pushing forward even when I didn't know how I would make it. Each struggle taught me something new about myself, about God, and His faithfulness.

I found strength in the very things that seemed to be breaking me. I learned that it was okay to feel weak, but I didn't have to stay there. God was with me in every moment, lifting me when I couldn't stand on my own.

Through the struggles, I discovered the power of resilience. I learned to get back up when life knocked me down, knowing that with God's help, I could face whatever came my way. The struggles I faced were not in vain. They were stepping stones on my path to greater things.

> **REFLECTION**
>
> *2 Corinthians 4:8-9 reminds us that struggles are a part of life, but they do not have to defeat us. Through Christ, we can find strength even in our weakest moments. Our struggles are not signs of failure—they are opportunities to grow, to strengthen our faith, and to draw closer to God.*

CHAPTER 14
Walking in Faith

"For we walk by faith, not by sight."

2 Corinthians 5:7

Faith is the foundation of my life. As a child, I was taught to trust in God and His promises, even when I couldn't see the way forward. There were times when my circumstances seemed impossible, and the future felt uncertain. But it was in those moments that I realized how important it was to walk by faith and not by sight.

2 Corinthians 5:7 tells us, *"For we walk by faith, not by sight."* This scripture became a guiding principle in my life. I learned that faith is not just a belief in God, it is a way of life. It is the confidence that God is working in our lives, even when we can't see the immediate results.

For many years, I struggled with feeling inadequate and uncertain about my future. My journey through school had not been easy, and there were countless times when

I doubted my abilities. But it was in those times of doubt that God reminded me to walk by faith.

Faith means trusting that God's plan is better than our own. It means believing that He is leading us, even when we don't understand the path. I learned to step out in faith, knowing that God would provide the strength, wisdom, and guidance I needed for each step.

Walking in faith didn't mean that I had all the answers. It didn't mean that the road was always smooth or easy. But it meant that I was trusting in the One who knew the way. Even when I didn't have the confidence to move forward, I learned to rely on God's promises and His perfect timing.

I realized that walking in faith is not about having everything figured out; it's about trusting God to lead us, even when the road is uncertain. It's about taking the next step, even when we can't see what's ahead. And it's about knowing that with God, we are never alone.

REFLECTION

2 Corinthians 5:7 teaches us that faith is not about our circumstances, it's about trusting in God's guidance, even when we can't see the full picture. Walking by faith means believing that God is always with us, leading us through each step of our journey.

CHAPTER 15
Overcoming Fear

> *"For God has not given us a spirit of fear, but of power and love and a sound mind."*
>
> **2 Timothy 1:7**

Fear is something that has plagued me at various points in my life. Fear of failure, fear of not measuring up, fear of being rejected, these fears would often hold me back from taking steps forward. But over the years, I've learned that fear is not from God. God has given us a spirit of power, love, and a sound mind, as we read in 2 Timothy 1:7.

For much of my life, fear seemed to be a constant companion. When I struggled in school, I feared that I would never succeed. I feared that my label as someone with learning difficulties would define me forever. The fear of being different and not fitting in held me back from fully embracing who I was.

But as I grew in my faith and understanding, I realized that fear is a lie. It tries to convince us that we are incapable, unworthy, and unable to achieve our dreams. But God's Word tells us otherwise. We are not given a spirit of fear, but one of power, love, and a sound mind.

I remember the first time I faced my fear head-on. I had been invited to speak at a women's event, and the thought of standing in front of a crowd terrified me. I questioned whether I was qualified, whether my story mattered, and whether anyone would listen. But I knew that God had called me to share my testimony, and I had to trust that He would give me the strength to do it.

I prayed for courage, and God answered. As I stepped onto that stage, all of my fears seemed to melt away. I realized that I wasn't relying on my strength—I was relying on God's power, and with His help, I could do anything.

Overcoming fear isn't a one-time victory; it's a daily choice. Every time fear rises, I remind myself of God's promises and choose to walk in faith, knowing that His power is greater than any fear.

> **REFLECTION**
>
> *2 Timothy 1:7 reminds us that fear does not come from God. When fear tries to hold us back, we can remember that God has given us the power, love, and sound mind to overcome it. By trusting in His strength, we can face any challenge that comes our way.*

CHAPTER 16
Living with Purpose

> *"For I know the plans I have for you," declares the Lord, "plans to prosper you and not to harm you, plans to give you a hope and a future."*
>
> **Jeremiah 29:11**

Living with purpose has been a driving force in my life. When I was younger, I often wondered what my purpose was. It felt like I was just going through the motions—going to school, dealing with struggles, trying to fit in, and trying to make sense of my identity. I didn't understand why I faced the challenges I did, and I often questioned what it all meant. But through prayer, faith, and reflection, I came to understand that God had a purpose for me all along.

Jeremiah 29:11 reminds us that God has plans for our lives, plans to prosper us and give us hope. When I reflect on this scripture, I am reminded that our purpose is not something we stumble upon by chance, it is woven into the very fabric of our lives by the Creator Himself. Each trial, each moment of struggle, each victory, and each setback has been a part of His plan to shape us into who He wants us to be.

For much of my early life, I couldn't see the purpose in my struggles. I questioned why I had to go through so much difficulty in school, why I had to be placed in special education, and why it seemed like I was always one step behind. But now I understand that those experiences were part of God's preparation for me. They gave me a heart of compassion, resilience, and determination.

I learned that my purpose wasn't defined by the labels others placed on me or the challenges I faced, it was defined by God. His plan for me was always bigger than my circumstances.

Living with purpose means seeking God's will for our lives, trusting that He is guiding us, and being open to the opportunities He places in front of us. It means understanding that every step we take is part of the journey that leads us closer to fulfilling His plans for us.

In every season of my life, I've strived to live with purpose, knowing that God's plans for me are greater than anything I could have imagined. My purpose isn't just about me, it's about using my life to bring glory to God and to help others.

> **REFLECTION**
>
> *Jeremiah 29:11 reminds us that God's plans for our lives are filled with hope and a future. We are not here by accident, and our struggles do not define our worth. Living with purpose means trusting God's plan, walking in His will, and using our gifts and experiences to serve others and fulfill His calling in our lives.*

CHAPTER 17
The Beauty of Forgiveness

> *"Be kind and compassionate to one another, forgiving each other, just as in Christ God forgave you."*
>
> **Ephesians 4:32**

Forgiveness is one of the most powerful gifts we can give, both to others and to ourselves. It is something that I have learned to value deeply over the years. When I was younger, I didn't fully understand the importance of forgiveness. It seemed difficult, especially when I felt wronged or hurt. But as I grew in my faith, I began to see forgiveness in a new light.

Ephesians 4:32 reminds us to be kind and compassionate, forgiving each other just as Christ forgave us. That is the standard we are called to live by. But forgiveness is not always easy. It can be especially hard when someone has hurt us deeply or when we've been mistreated. Yet, the freedom that comes with forgiveness is worth the challenge.

I remember a time when I struggled with forgiving someone who had wronged me. The hurt and disappointment weighed heavily on my heart. But over time, I realized that holding on to that pain only kept me bound. It was only when I chose to forgive that I began to feel the weight lifting off of me.

Forget the hurt or excuse the wrongs done to us. It simply means that we release the hold that those wrongs have over us. We choose to let go of bitterness and resentment, trusting that God will heal our hearts.

When we forgive, we reflect the love and grace of God. Just as He forgives us when we fall short, we are called to extend that same forgiveness to others. This act of kindness and compassion opens the door to healing and restoration in our relationships.

Over the years, I've experienced firsthand how forgiveness can transform lives. It doesn't just mend relationships with others, it also brings peace to our own hearts. The beauty of forgiveness is that it frees us to move forward, to embrace healing, and to walk in the love of Christ.

REFLECTION

Ephesians 4:32 calls us to forgive others just as God has forgiven us. Forgiveness is not always easy, but it is always necessary. It brings freedom, healing, and peace, and it reflects the love and grace of God. Let go of bitterness and choose forgiveness—it will transform your heart and your relationships.

CHAPTER 18
Embracing God's Timing

> *"To everything there is a season, and a time for every matter under heaven."*
>
> **Ecclesiastes 3:1**

One of the most challenging aspects of my journey has been learning to embrace God's timing. As humans, we tend to want everything now, immediate results, immediate answers, and immediate solutions. But God's timing is different from ours, and I've come to realize that trusting in His timing is one of the greatest acts of faith.

Ecclesiastes 3:1 teaches us that *"To everything there is a season, and a time for every matter under heaven."* This reminds us that everything in life happens in its own time. There are moments in life when we want things to move faster, when we feel like we should be further along in our journey, but God's plan unfolds in perfect timing.

When I was younger, I was frustrated by the delays in my life. I wanted to be "successful" quickly. I wanted to prove to others, and to myself, that I was capable. I looked around and saw peers advancing in their careers, their families, their lives, and I felt left behind. But in time, I realized that comparison and impatience only created unnecessary stress.

God's plan for my life is unique. His timing is intentional, and His pace is perfect. I learned that it's not about rushing toward an end goal, it's about trusting that God has a purpose for every season, every delay, and every challenge.

Looking back, I can see how every step, every delay and every obstacle, was part of God's preparation for me. His timing allowed me to grow, learn, and develop the character needed for the next season of my life. What felt like setbacks were opportunities to build resilience, patience, and dependence on Him.

Embracing God's timing means trusting that He knows what's best for us. It means learning to wait with faith, knowing that He is working ~~in~~ for us, even when we can't see the full picture.

REFLECTION

Ecclesiastes 3:1 teaches us that everything has a season, and God is in control of the timing. Instead of rushing ahead or growing impatient, trust that God's timing is perfect. Every moment of waiting, every delay, and every season has a purpose, and in God's time, everything will come to fruition.

CHAPTER 19
Strength in Weakness

> *"But he said to me, 'My grace is sufficient for you, for my power is made perfect in weakness.' Therefore, I will boast all the more gladly of my weaknesses, so that the power of Christ may rest upon me."*
>
> **2 Corinthians 12:9**

Strength in weakness is one of the most profound lessons I've learned in my life. When I was younger, I saw my weaknesses as something to be ashamed of. I thought that my struggles in school, my inability to meet certain expectations, and my challenges in learning were signs of failure. I believed that being weak meant being inadequate. But as I grew in my relationship with God, I came to realize that my weakness was a place where His power could shine through.

In 2 Corinthians 12:9, Paul tells us that God's grace is sufficient for us, and His power is made perfect in our weakness. This was a revelation that changed my perspective. I realized that it's not in our strengths that God's power is most evident, it's in our weaknesses. When we are weak, we are more reliant on God, and that's where His strength can truly be displayed.

I look back on my journey and see how my moments of weakness were the very places where God worked the most. When I struggled in school, God provided the strength to keep going. When I doubted my abilities, He reminded me that my worth wasn't tied to my performance.

There's a certain humility that comes with acknowledging our weakness. It's not about feeling defeated, it's about recognizing that we need God in every area of our lives. When we humble ourselves and admit our need for Him, that's when His strength becomes most evident.

God doesn't call us to be perfect. He calls us to surrender. In our weaknesses, we find His grace. In our struggles, we experience His strength. Through every trial and difficulty, God shows us that He is enough.

> **REFLECTION**
>
> *2 Corinthians 12:9 reminds us that God's power is made perfect in our weakness. Instead of hiding our struggles, we can embrace them, knowing that God's grace is sufficient. Our weaknesses become opportunities for His strength to be displayed, and in our vulnerability, we find His power.*

CHAPTER 20
Walking in Victory

"But thanks be to God, who gives us the victory through our Lord Jesus Christ."

1 Corinthians 15:57

Walking in victory has been one of the most powerful aspects of my journey, but it hasn't always been easy to understand what true victory is. For much of my life, I thought victory meant achieving success, receiving recognition, or overcoming every challenge without struggle. But through my experiences and the guidance of God, I have come to realize that true victory is not measured by earthly standards, it is found in our relationship with Jesus Christ.

1 Corinthians 15:57 reminds us that *"thanks be to God, who gives us the victory through our Lord Jesus Christ."* The victory we walk in is not of our own making but through Christ. This victory is the assurance of knowing that no matter what we face in this life, we are more than conquerors through Him.

My journey hasn't been without its challenges. I've faced setbacks, disappointments, and moments when I felt like giving up. But through it all, I've learned that victory doesn't mean avoiding difficulties, it means overcoming them with God's strength. It means having the courage to keep moving forward, even when the path is unclear or when I don't have all the answers.

Victory is knowing that in every season of life, God is with us. He walks alongside us through every trial, and His presence gives us the strength to endure. Victory is not about avoiding pain, but about experiencing God's faithfulness in the midst of it.

I have learned that victory is also about having peace in the storm. It's about trusting that God is working on all things together for our good, even when we can't see how. The victory we have in Christ is the assurance that He is in control and that nothing can separate us from His love.

In walking in victory, I've also learned that it's not about us, it's about using our victories to serve others and bring glory to God. When we experience God's victory in our lives, we are called to share that victory with others, to encourage them, and to help them see the hope and strength that comes through Christ.

REFLECTION

1 Corinthians 15:57 reminds us that victory comes through Christ. True victory is not about avoiding struggles but about walking through them with God's strength. It's about trusting in His faithfulness, knowing that He gives us the victory. As we walk in this victory, we are called to share it with others, bringing hope and glory to God's name.

ENCOURAGING PARENTS TO PUSH THEIR CHILDREN TO A GOOD FUTURE

As parents, we play a crucial role in shaping the future of our children. It's our responsibility to nurture their potential, guide them, and provide the love and support they need to thrive. One of the most important things we can do is to push our children, not in a forceful or overwhelming way, but in a way that encourages them to reach beyond what they think is possible for themselves.

I have seen firsthand the power of encouragement and support from my parents. My mother's unwavering belief in me kept me going, even when I didn't believe in myself. She saw potential in me that I couldn't see, and that's what gave me the strength to push through the obstacles.

YOLANDA HILL

ENCOURAGING PARENTS TO INSPIRE THEIR CHILDREN IN SCHOOL

The Power of Parental Encouragement

Parents, you are the first and most important teachers in your child's life. Before they ever step into a classroom, they learn from you—how to speak, how to behave, how to navigate life's challenges. Your encouragement and support set the foundation for their confidence and success in school.

Some children struggle in school, not because they lack intelligence, but because they lack belief in themselves. That belief comes from you. When you tell your child, "I believe in you," those words become a source of strength. When you push them to try again after failure, you teach them resilience. When you celebrate their efforts, even when they don't get perfect grades, you show them that growth is more important than perfection.

Education is not just about grades; it's about developing character, discipline, and perseverance.

Encourage your child to give their best effort, not just in academics but in their attitude toward learning. Remind them that knowledge is power and that every lesson learned is a step toward their future success.

OVERCOMING CHALLENGES TOGETHER

School can be difficult for many children. Some struggle with reading, math, or making friends. Others may feel pressure to succeed or fear failure. As parents, you have the power to help your child navigate these challenges by being present, patient, and proactive.

If your child is struggling academically, don't let them give up. Instead, find ways to support them. Sit with them while they do their homework, help them develop study habits, and connect with their teachers for guidance. Let them know that struggling doesn't mean they aren't smart—it means they are learning.

Encourage open conversations about school. Ask them about their day, their favorite subjects, and what they find difficult. If they express frustration or discouragement, listen with understanding. Your support reassures them that they are not alone in their journey.

And most importantly, remind them that their worth is not defined by their grades. Teach them to aim for excellence, but also to learn from mistakes. Success is not about never failing—it's about never giving up.

INSTILLING A GROWTH MINDSET

A growth mindset is the belief that intelligence and abilities can be developed through effort, persistence, and learning. Teaching your child this mindset will empower them to embrace challenges rather than fear them.

Instead of saying, "I can't do this," encourage them to say, "I can't do this yet, but I will keep trying." Instead of fearing mistakes, teach them to see mistakes as opportunities to improve. When they struggle, remind them that even the most successful people faced obstacles—but they didn't quit.

Celebrate progress, no matter how small. If your child improves their reading skills, praise their effort. If they solve a difficult math problem, acknowledge their determination. When children see that hard work leads to improvement, they become motivated to keep going.

Help them set goals for themselves. Whether it's improving in a subject, reading a book, or learning a new skill, setting and achieving goals builds confidence and self-discipline. Let them know that success is a journey, and every step forward is an achievement.

BEING A ROLE MODEL AND SUPPORT SYSTEM

Children learn more from what we do than what we say. If we want them to value education, we must show them that learning is a lifelong journey. Share stories of your own challenges and successes. Let them see you reading, learning new skills, or working toward your goals. When they see that growth never stops, they will be inspired to continue learning.

Be involved in their education. Attend parent-teacher conferences, celebrate their achievements, and stay informed about their progress. Show them that their education matters to you.

Above all, remind them that they are capable, loved, and supported. Your words have the power to shape their future. Tell them:

- "You are smart and capable."
- "I am proud of your hard work."
- "Keep going—you can do it!"
- "No matter what, I will always support you."

When children know they have parents who believe in them, they will have the confidence to face any

challenge, reach for their dreams, and achieve greatness. Final Words to Parents:

Your encouragement is the foundation of your child's success. Speak life into their dreams, push them to do their best, and remind them that no obstacle is too big when they believe in themselves. With your support, your child will not only succeed in school but will also develop the courage and resilience to succeed in life.

RESOURCES

Holy Bible, King James Version (KJV)

ABOUT THE AUTHOR

YOLANDA HILL

Yolanda R. Hill was born and raised in Jersey City, New Jersey. As the eldest of eleven children, she developed a deep love and appreciation for family, cherishing the bonds with her brothers, sisters, and beloved parents.

A dedicated and passionate learner, Yolanda graduated from high school in 1993. She continued her education at Denmark Technical College in South Carolina, where she earned an Associate's Degree in Early

Childhood Education. Determined to further her knowledge and impact in the field of education, she later obtained a Bachelor's Degree in Educational Studies from Grand Canyon University.

Yolanda's journey reflects her commitment to education, family, and personal growth. She remains devoted to making a difference in the lives of children and inspiring others through her dedication and experience.

www.ingramcontent.com/pod-product-compliance
Lightning Source LLC
LaVergne TN
LVHW061556070526
838199LV00077B/7079